BODY RITES
(beyond the darkening)

OTHER WORKS BY ARNOLD H ITWARU

Poetry

Shattered Songs
The Sacred Presence
entombed survivals

Fiction

Shanti

Scholarly

Mass Communication and Mass Deception
Critiques of Power
The Invention of Canada

BODY RITES
(beyond the darkening)

Arnold H Itwaru

TSAR
Toronto
1991

The Publishers acknowledge generous assistance from
the Ontario Arts Council and the Canada Council.

Cover art and design by Natasha Ksonzek.

Copyright © 1991 by Arnold H Itwaru.

Except for purposes of review, no part
of this publication may be reproduced, in any form,
without prior permission of the publishers.

ISBN 0-920661-17-3

TSAR Publications
P.O. Box 6996, Station A
Toronto, Ontario, Canada
M5W 1X7

This work returns to some of the presences of my reflection and finds in the anguished footpaths of these poems changing utterances out of which other meditations arise and join the moments of this present volume.

When the actions of nation-states rewrite themselves in the gruesome ecstasies of the day poetry must rethink its body in whose corporeality we fearfully dream.

A H Itwaru

ACKNOWLEDGEMENTS

Some of these poems appeared in modified form and context in *The Toronto South Asian Review*, *India in the Caribbean*, *Artrage*, *Shattered Songs,* and *entombed survivals.*

Thank you, Ontario Arts Council in providing financial assistance for the completion of this book.

A H Itwaru

For Natasha, this bleeding heave of strangled silence, today in eternity

...of life of breath, bearer, begotten and born in light, sky-earth lake, worrier, knower...
Popol Vuh

...in the sowing of the seeding earth, in the dawning of growth and life, in the sowing of the sun and moon and stars, in the sowing in the womb and the dawning of birth, in the sowing of death and the dawning of light in darkness....
Popol Vuh

Contents

where do you go 1
your face 2
and i have come 3
these painful chambers 5
watcher 6
looking at our bodies 7
tonight 8
here and there 9
this mirror 11
you shatter my river's mirror 12
and in this carnival 14
drenched they break the sky 15
among the lilies 16
in this drum 17
we who have survived birth 18
sacred presence 19
fresh water pain 22
perfect 24
perhaps this is merely a play 25
arrival 27
stops 28
snake 29
i remember 30
waiting 31
they return again 32
entombed survivals (nine movements) 33
matin mornings 55
gently now gently 56
changing return 57
house 58
drought 59
visit 60
greeting 63
body rites (thirteen chants) 65

where do you go

where do you go bleeding not seen
wailing not heard
where do you go shadow of my shadow
watching blinded
what perversity lurks in the edges of the hour

who goes there dreaming my dream

your face

your face asks what i cannot give
your loneliness my tears
your anger my sorrow
your pain my hurt
i have abandoned you, you say

we are standing at the doorway
and i do not want to leave
yet each time i do
i leave hiding my face lest you see me weep

each time our eyes embrace the embrace we
did not share, our silence a pain
we dare not speak

i leave you now
i always leave
always this rush this gulf between us
yet i have never left

and i have come

and i have come
and now i must go
and the apple tree will bloom
and the door, this door i now face
will open to the warmth of the roses
in whose dream of summer we lived

i will leave these birds
whose plumed waiting beats
in the silence of this table
where we have fed and loved
in the breath of our breathing

this has been an antechamber of crescendos
arias and sonatas i have come to
where we dwelt as the snow melted
and the garden called
where you worked and i dreamed

i do not want to go
but i must
i leave not knowing where i'm going
i leave
i have to
but yes the winter has been bearable

i go but i cannot leave
i go leaving me here
i go taking you with me
i go ever returning

so short this season in which i grew
in the sounds and silences of this place–
the creaking of the floor

the crackle of flame in the fire
the muted flow of water in the night

the door has often resisted my locking of it
but perhaps moreso it was i who did not want to face
its locking which locks me out

i did not want to
i did not want to

between night entrances have we met
have talked in the rise of each *chakra*
in each violin's mournful pleasure
in the joy of gongs cymbals and ancient horns
in the eternal coming in which i now go

these painful chambers

these painful chambers inhabit
the windows i open and close each day
these indifferent doors of habit
stained in the fading glass of another time

these hallways repeat the illusion of intent
in our rituals of undress and concealment
our movement from here to there
as we place things and remove them
use them
lose them
replace them
in the alien recurrences of our doing

these rooms are zones of non and not–
dissembling silences against the structured decor
of dying light
the enigma of padded floors and hard bare words
walled in unmeetings

watcher

i watched him wrestle with the soil
reaping illusive yesterdays

pieces of rubble   broken stone
offer themselves   his back bowed to the sun
clapboard houses against the sea
and tattered wash in an empty sky

an old man   dim in the threatening wind
he collects his wash   stores himself
and disappears

looking at our bodies

we're ashamed no longer to undress before each other
we let the years' passing acknowledge our knowing

once modesty made you avert your eyes and cover your breasts
but now after the seasons
we shuffle out of our clothes
accustomed to our bodies' silent testimony

the nights do our dreaming for us
as we grow under this vague sky's lustre
with so little learned   so much to know

twenty years from now   perhaps alone as we started
we'll embrace the dark
too embarrassed to bear our bodies' witness
and under courteous sheets resurrect distant afternoons
to take us a while from the knowledge of our corruption

tonight

tonight there is no rush   we watch aspens
shivering against the stars   even the loons are
listening to the silence

yesterday it rained and tonight my words die
with the last embers of this fire we both made

for a while   for this moment everything seems fine

here and there

here clocks explode, faces shatter
eternal ash
burned out bodies
word to ash
burned out voices
act to ash
the liar God
the liar the Devil
the liar the tumescent explosion of Leaders' pustulent tongues
the bombs and ecstasy of high-tech efficiencies
peace that passeth all understanding

here among the shadows darkness invents itself in the laboratoried light
in ecstatic coffined anthems and transports
of killing empire-order-pride
moralizing majority applauses and speeches and applauses
and speeches and applauses
devout domestic convictions
peace that passeth all understanding

here lies explode in the crematoriums of streets villages and towns there
how like christmas lights the cities blaze, the bomber says, smiling
away from the mothers and fathers the children murdered in sleep
his Mission's Surgical-sweet efficient strike

it happens over there far away from here
where children are taught to hope and pray it's all going to be over soon
and Daddy will come marching home to the sound of trumpet and drum

they must not ask
how many children in your brave and heroic deeds have you killed there
O brave and patriotic Daddy dear

they must say
tell me how good and right it felt when you bombed the Enemy
Daddy dear, my hero, my man of action, my strongman, my love, my maker of the new world in whose order I will be safe

peace that passeth all understanding
from cars to tanks to missiles of patriotic zeal
milk and oil and blood for special effects
ships and planes and Smart Bombs
another video game between meals
between orgasms and Commanders' strategic talk
and Weapons Systems acclamations
the new order
Prime Time Killing
a Family Affair
a national ecstasy
a patriotic movie about good and bad
over popcorn Pepsi and Coca Cola
and other instant feasts to "ZAP snack attacks"
here
far from there
peace
peace that passeth all understanding

this mirror

this mirror has forgotten me
room of dead smiles decrepit dawns
weeping too chafed and brittle for my touch

not me

yet corrosive
no longer simple
this inner eye knows subterranean assassinations
corpses' crepuscular incoherent dreams whose crackling wake
sends me cowering in the shifting rooms of yesterday

these rooms wait
they watch
they see my voice smear my face
they've seen this before
they're the museums of my unforgetting

inside
inside the inside of my inside
i strike out
i hack at them
i try to tear them out of me
but they move easily
they watch the anguished fall of my withered rage
they float like blazing barges
and it is i who ebbing away carries them still

you shatter my river's mirror

you shatter my river's mirror
and my shore is now a lie
currents eddies undertows in me

you come in a circle of ravens
my sky my river my shore in your eyes

i ask of you nothing
i give nothing
i do not know what has happened to the stillness
which one grew here

you live in the echo of each leaf
each bark i bark
imitating the gateposts of speech

a dream a pulse which will not die will not go
you fold and unfold each day
you imitate me so completely

umbilicus hour
omen hour
the valley of the shadow of death
not the dream i dream and do not dream
out here mice teeth are on the bread
maggots in the cursed mud
snakes in my path hissing death
filth and blood in holy places
not the dream i dream and do not dream

umbilicus hour
a tug a snap of instant evenings
scrambled bleeps and heroes and idols
who vanish and ever vanish

hour of light and speed and high places–
how have we grown–
the mice the maggots the snake
are in the hall the kitchen the bed
they watch in silence behind the empty wall
the fluid screens of pleasure

the neighbours nod and smile
all is well

and in this carnival

and in this carnival you offer me
the drunkenness of fire
an earful of drums
a dance in my blood

your face sweats anthems you do not know
your tongue flames the night of my uneasy watch
as you dance you weave you slide past
you return in an applause of bondage
so sweet in our eyes

we have performed
how well have we performed
and now
this stage imprisons us once more

serpent human demon
once more we dance within the barriers of flames,
the audience adores us

we are this carnival are we

drenched they break the sky

drenched they break the sky
their loins a tyranny of weather
their children's memory: flotsam, harbours, barbarous horizons

daily we meet
unfold
drift
return
daily the ruined stone listens

daily wrinkled
uneasily naked
abandoned
unforgiven
unforgiving
daily the pulse the blood the dream severed

among the lilies

among the lilies, shy petals once delicate and tremulous
mantras and madigrals in the temples of heaven
Mother, milk on my tongue

Mother, amidst the rubble of sun
and daughters and sons in bamboo barbed wire and mud
Mother, in the eaves of night
mortal clay mortal earth poisoned
do you see how the vulture caws before it too is devoured

Mother, on my child's smile a brow of blood congeals the
lamentations of dusk
the madness at noon that cannot be forgiven
this child my child
whose shadow dances in hope lost in hope
in the pulse of my fathering

Mother, where do we go
what can we say has happened
what will happen to us?

in this drum

in this drum eternal our footfall
the flute of our breath drawn
in the blooming closures of
each rice-grown mud-grown unremembering

in this drum oceans and distance converge and depart
in the frozen luminosities which threaten our silences
and the dreams that dream us in the hurrying streets
and alien shores of our eyes

inflamed in this drum the agony of our skin
is stretched against the beating heart of sleep
our children's innocence this side of tomorrow
beyond the darkening
this morning of their play

in this drum our silence knows
the lamentations each dawn and each dusk
there and always here in us
each sad flute of gongs and bells
in the flicker of our breathing

knows the rooms and houses of private betrayals
publicly denied
the dying within this killing peace
this season of yet another order
ordering death and death and death as life

in this drum we go greeting faces we think we know
distant echoes and pulses
lips that smile in blooming closures
and smiling fade and fade away

we who have survived birth

we who have survived birth
and for whom the distance lengthens and closes in
for whom the pangs of desire will not bloom again
at the end of speeches in the halls of lofty intent
nor in these days of poisoned rain air words water
needled in the vein
in the jungles and deserts in the cities and the villages
echoing a terrible peace

we have survived birth
bearer of fear bearer of hope bearer of joy
hater hated hating
bearer of rage and love
loving
killing
dying
we have survived birth

we have survived survival
survived
we are the survived

we are the surviving whose survival we sek beyond the mined
corridors   broken streets and homes
worn smiles' necroptic masks
death at the ports and terminals of hope
factories of casual assassinations
beyond
beyond beyond

beyond where silence ends the rush that breaks the night in eyes
in mouth in hands in loins in rock in sky
in water of us watered of our watering
where silence ends where we celebrate

sacred presence

i have come by the flat-bottomed boat
backwoods snakes the vulture's seasons
where you return with blood-drawn face burnt skin and the smell
of defeat in your loins

i who rose to birth in you
i who escaped in rooms in cities in continents
in dreams that drift away
in this other darkening

i have come by your grave unmarked unearthed
and i have paid my respects
i have buried you at the foot of night
the mango tree seen at last and no more

by dewdrop by leaf by bud by tears i have come
where the jasmine no longer assails the appletree orangetree
guavabush peppertree dawn

by the brick of bombed out roadways have i come
infested canals swamps streams and rivers
bridges above the alligator's cold-blooded wait
the mule-chain jangle of harnesses and voices
lime-rum balm useless pills and potions
dry rain
calabash skulls
asthma
ague in the noonday heat

i have come in the cursed mud
the thunder the lightning which mends the dark again
and splits apart the ancient tree
where the wind in gusts of choked lament sings

the gate you intended to fix hangs askew
the sweetbush vine lies withered in the barbed-wire fence
the dog howls at shadows which hover here forever

the house your house our home inhabits strangers
but the wounded evening lives in the solitary arch of your brow
fields from which your long gaze returns
reined in the falling of the night and my silence

yesterday we talked we worked we ate we quarrelled
yesterday there was no messenger

the door is empty the messenger gone
he the faceless One who comes in the nether hour
who deposits in the aperture of this rented confinement
my unwanted text of grief

between yesterday and you and me
the rain fell the light fell in mornings of parched throat
burning eyes and streets which lead to humiliation

between us, Death, improvident distancer has forever dislodged
seeing
between us the ashen obliterator reigns

i have descended
and risen in the shrines of sacred gongs and ceremonies
shifting forms and voices which vanish with no answer

by the villages of rubble ragblown have i risen
by broken plough and hunger-drawn flesh
by the barnyard cackle of dying voices
by the buckling bridge of shrunken bone and hope
by the oceans' edges where children build and the tide
obliterates in an infinitesima of sand and water

by the whispers of trees and fields
by the soft low singing of lotus-grown water
by the morning bell of children's voices which strike and strike

in the tolling of their play

by shadowed paths beneath a brambled sky
by protuberant roots
by ripe fallen fruit
by the shimmering breathe of light in seedling green
by winter rot in the bone
by sudden embraces
here where the morning has gone
where the dust has risen
here in this lunacy of
heat and light
and dark

fresh water pain

fresh water pain
whose illusion i am
an indentured present i want and do not want
and have become
and have not

a delirium of remembered branches across the woodsmoke dreaming
dusk
across flights by land and water and air
dark voice in the labourings of the morning's fall into night

middle-passaged
passing
beneath the colouring of desire
in the enemy's eye
a scatter of words and broken wishes in Shiva's dance

uprooted
we have survived the piercing morning
we have survived death in the backdams and hovels of hope
we have survived we who know the snake's fangs
the tides' and seasons' treachery
the boot the fist the spit of the British Empire

we have survived the breakage of speech
language which formulates us
in its curse

our men are proud
they bear handsomely the garments of their imprisonment

our women awaken desire
cosmeticized and clothed in the imaginings

of their exploiter

a parade of painted voices
in the lachrimatories of mirrors and anguished silences
in the Other's echo and call

the forgotten dead struck down in life
the lamentations in the villages and firesides
the weed-grown places of burial and hope
we have survived

indenture lives in dates and distances
not in the antic dance we dance
speech which speaks our death in postures of greed and denial
pain which strikes in the striking of each stricken hour

where is he, the gentle one
taken to the fields
who never returned

where is she, mother of my tongue
who wept and toiled
and is no more

and this child this youth
whose eyes do not reach me
whose speech i dread
how will he fare in these labyrinths which lengthen and lengthen
in their unopening

perfect

bound
nailed
wide eyes unseeing
straw ghosts
bodies

the pulse hungry for touch is quietly strangled

no flame
no desire
shapes that move in dressed decorum
make sounds

perfect

perhaps this is merely a play

perhaps this is merely a play
a smile a breath a shudder of shadows
a howl of echoes
fire becoming the speech of the human mouth
the spaces of silence in the hearing of the ears
the serenity of the moon within the chaos of sun
before the final entrance

veiled the dreamers dance
they dance their dream in loins of blood and sacrifice
pleasure's dreaded secret

builder of altar and shrine
monuments of memory
that lead to the solemn silence amidst plots of awe
and buried pain alive for a while

demons and angels
the deaths we abhor   run from   commit

here in this universe of contrived night
death is an anonymous tale
someone else's winter
we merely watch

watch
wash our hands in words
in the distillation of ceremonies and mystic cantos
dreaming of Elysium

there are no violations
the dancers dream
their dance falling like the fireworks of yesteryear
the play is only a play

in it the beast leaps
hounded in voices
the beast leaps and roars
confused
cursed upright
dreaming of eternity in a howl of echoes
terrified

arrival

this is the place
mark its name
the streets you must learn to remember

there are special songs here
they do not sing of you
in them you do not exist
but to exist you must learn to love them
you must believe them when they say
there are no sacrificial lambs here

the houses are warm
there's bread there's wine

bless yourself
you have arrived

        listen
keys   rattle
locks   click
doors   slam
        silence

stops

in the slats in the cities
between oceans and continents
i am your me crying in the darkness of burning yesterday
yet i'm not

in silence afloat
i am a voyage of water and wind
yet i'm not

a fissure of music in the cracks of night
i am and i am not
a wandering pulse in the abysm of dream
i am i am i'm not
i remember and do not remember

you can see my body bending
arching itself opening in giving
perhaps you can
perhaps you still can

in silence afloat
i burst in flashes and am swallowed
in the labyrinths of light

snake

i watch the snake move

it has shifting eyes
it knows its world its crag kingdom
its belly upon the yielding ground of its serpentine

it stops in a shadow
coils
begins to sing

i watch it grow arms legs faces
in an aria of madrigals and litanies i've known all along

i watch me embrace it

it attacks

i remember

i remember smoke under blazing skies
fields and beaches where skeletons eat the sand
my father struck down in his house
mother buried there somewhere
blizzards of bodies
strangled cries by the fence where the cat haunted the boundaries
of the morning   i remember
yet like smoke like smoke i float
i flow from dream to dream

the child i thought i had left haunts me
crying
wailing
smothered in silence

he will not be consoled and half of my life is over
floating
still running
kicking
screaming
i who have tried to mend fences
to fix my roof
to nail things down

the pulse hurled against my doorway is someone else's placenta
the presences in my rooms of living are someone else's dream

they have followed the many masks i've worn
and they wait to drink me up

will dawn one day before this
answer all my questions
or will i wonder why is it i have ever lived

waiting

in my bone its raining
in my flesh it is snowing
in my brain the sun's kite is severed

i dance in the veiled rim of the moon
stone eyes dust drowned
loins already rehearsed
where no one meets

across this stage you sit
while i puzzle over distant smiles and laughter
the fires in the thickets of your eyes

knowing we have been words
hollow presences across this dais of our meeting

i listen outstretched
waiting
as if waiting for you
waiting

they return again

across the long sands dreamers build castles
rulers live in them
armies knock them down

across the long sands the stranded kelp's litany
of deserter tides
frozen waters breaking the horizon
holding the sky

they proliferate in snow gardens
they petrify the forest
they blow away like rubble
they return again

entombed survivals

(movement one)

it is the time is it not
the hammering of the heart offered to leaders and god
the solstice of the body
the edge of the stairs falling from the wings of Babel

time of the priest the murderer the leader the saint
time of just deeds and sacrifice
time of the storm hurled against the desert of wounded lungs
lava and generosity escapes and imprisonment

time of the blazing cloud
tears ground in our loins
love wept in parting
time to hold you for a moment forever

forever across this broken river
tufts of hair
this bombed out home
ash of flesh
in the temples and palaces of prayer and justice

forever across sacral borders
chains and crystal nights
i call
to touch your glance which leaps in flames

across flailings in bombs in violins
in dead eyes collecting indifferent heaven
across our backward forward backward glancing
across the bloodpaths of precision and efficiency

my light of darkness my burning sun
the voices slain have vanished in so many words

the bodies strewn there are someone else's yesterday

who sees now blinded by words and other noises
who lives now bearing all creation
whose effluvium poisons earth and sky
what pretext hangs about the doorsteps and lawns
and secret chambers draped in freedom

who sees amidst the bedrooms of the blinded morning
where speech speaks softly speaking death
where speech screams and is silenced

in the cities in the houses in the principalities
something devours words devouring us
something watches
waits and watches as waiting we kneel before this altar

the word
this confessional
the word
this alliance
the word

kneel
prostrate ourselves
mortally wounded

wounding

weeping in pleasure
and weeping
immortal my mortal
we who ply the tides of blood and roses
we who gaze in the sad erection of armies and borders
we who bleed in each other's sleep

each breath you breathe is a moment of me
a fire in the dark
a burst of my blood

a scatter of ashes mounds and poppies
confessing everything and nothing

where i have stolen through the shadows of light
to glance at you
to appease a warm torture in so tortuous an hunger

each day laneways and corridors bring me chambers i do not know
each day i enter entering others
i tread across the dead drowned in a rubble of flowers and prayers

i enter these empires within the sun
these burning echoes in the undersides of my eyelids
where my unknown assailant wounds me at every turn

i know and do not know him
i know and do not know her
i know the contours of each wound
the marrow of each gash and burn i seek to heal
the ceremonies of torture a thousand thousand empires have formed

the dawn mourns the light of day
a shrouded corpse that breathes my breath
that dies each time we touch

i rise in this touch that kills
i seek this house's dizzy support
its beams' still centre
its ovens of silence

with shadowed eye and ancient mane my assailant stares
a beggar from the marketplaces and palaces
a perversity amidst the voices' fevered gleam
a withered tongue
a perversity in this sodden earth
this high-tech sweetness
ironic rainbows this solitary sun-drenched passing

entombed survivals

(movement two)

the leaves are turning you say
the trees will soon be bare
blood and gold and winter's sheet
the tangled clouds against my windowed dream
where you have painted me
and i have written you
where you have sung me
and i have screamed you
where you have touched me
and i have dreamed us
where the storm has burst
and the ground has cracked
where you vanish in nooks and crannies and oceans
in sunken dreams in sunken caverns
in storms in gales
and in silken waters
star to star
shore to shore
each dark sun's burning

the leaves turn and it   is night
it is night unknown and unknowing
it is night
it is night among the fissures the foothills the wrinkles
night among strangers
night
it is night
night among the phantoms on the edges of promise
night through the looking glass
where i enter winter in spring
frozen bones
phlegm in the blood
cities of snow

villages of cemeteries

the clock has struck leaving again our broken pier
the evening of our unentered house
your voice burnt on my tongue
morning of yesterday

yesterday the hibiscus bleeds another silence
as through the eaves the sleeping river heaves and sighs
yesterday the apple-tree crumbles of diseased fruit
there where the worm has eaten the fragrant guava
where burnt sugarcane rots in the skin and dream
of prayers and smiles
where lowered eyelids know the viper at the gate
the scorpion in the leaves
the siege of vision

yesterday under courteous sheets we resurrected
distant wishes and orgasms
the times we tried the times we failed

the faces in the street are fading
the bodies in the footpaths are vague
all the laneways have grown strange

entombed survivals

(movement three)

my door brings the din of rented promises i vow not to heed
i know their tenor their pitch their assaults
they offer me the embrace of sameness
faces of contrived caring impaled on electron screens
eye consuming mouth consuming hope
consuming

but O the word dies in the flame of the faroff dawn
the word dies in the faroff dawn of this fire i am obsessed to
make in the faroff dawn the word dies in a flame of shrapnel

the word dies
the word dies
in the faroff dawn the dusk has no memory
in the faroff dawn the word dies in wounds you and i know and do
not know

you and i know and do not know
the orgy behind the walls of politicoes and gunfire
where peace sits obedient in the corners of catacombs
and the labyrinths of mass graves
all warmth quelled

where it is calm
the doors and locks secure they say
where the agony and the dying
dressed in your own robe your armour
your livery of defeat
are accomplished in style

but in the tumultous shadow of our dreaming
two bodies are entering each other
two tongues are seeking and seeking

two moments unfurl
and another silence is born

take
dream
these are the echoes in the mountains and craters
a wailing on nameless graves
take
dream
you are more than a shadow on weary eyelids
more than an evening's lament
more than a wish hurled against vitriol and fire
immortal my mortal
more than forms moving on this earth of hope
more than a blindfold in this crossing
more than words mined in smiles
guarded in glitter
glossed over in toasts of wine and terror
sung out
sucked dry in jingles and marches
and speeches where victims never change

who will walk when the stone speaks and dreams again
will the night repeat and repeat the spectral pulse
fanged and thorned
scaled feet shaped in escapes

will the dawn repeat itself
bruised and sad
we who linger on the borders of hope

under the eaves of the sun we flow
we toss
we turn
we weep
we dance

dying
living

dying

for death and death are this season's seasoned season
the invented craters of volcanoes never dormant
never
the indulgences which promise promise
fetid dream in fetid sheets
a distant someone's distant distance
the wire's raucous rhythm
birth of noise that dies in noise
the fist against our eyes where the tyrant rages

but tonight the path that circles water and tree
transcends the cathedralled sky

in the shrine of our gaze
the lambent lanterns of moon and stars
dismiss the shadowed dream of fitful brows

the wind rehearses our phrases
dresses and dips into the river of night

entombed survivals

(movement four)

in the filling of a filling i dream
a fool recalling dusk perhaps
where yesterday hangs about the fields and ceilings
and windows float in the growing days
of flotsam-aches on tide-drawn beaches far away

in the silence of the evening
and in the pilgrimage of our gaze
in the dark blaze of the falling sun
in the centre of the tide's departure
and in the tide's return

in the sea-bed sky-bound tolling of the bell
i am your melody
your multitude
your multitude of me

yours among the incense and candles of denial
the dying in our weeping
the mantras and matins stained in hope
the word's flicker in the stillness
the book our body our text
our body our text our book

here above the sewers and factories
the cemeteries
the high places
above the poem you the poem me
cauldrons of schema schemata dogma
here inside
here outside
above
beneath

within
here oceans rush up to confuse

and standing here
this somewhere nowhere everywhere here
standing
watching you
i am mad all over again

mad in this moving stillness
i reach you reaching me
a faroff place i have known and never known
an ancient wandering shadow
a lamentation of drizzles and dewdrops
that fester over the hill where they take you each time

it is a night of precision here
cold air burning the nostrils of a furious sky
a night of dissection
desire
of tapestries and tapestries which haunt even in their illusion

night
my terror of light
mortal
immortal
my earth
my universe
my sob
my silence

the hour brings me shifting seas
i tilt and stagger in
horizons of salted edges which dissolve
and dissolve in the solitudes of my sleeping

the moans here are practised monodies
they eat the faces of their singers
they come within the gales in the paths behind the house

where i once left them
pebbles in a dry stream
the glow of forever against fields of rice
barbed wire
canals
gutters
rivers i thought always ran towards forgetting

afternoon holds me in the falling of the falling light
where you trace the boundaries of ink and distance
in the flicker of my unremembering

today i saw you in the womb of every town and village
through which i passed
you looked from the shadows from quiet lonely places
from windows which opened to the heavens

you gazed across fields of ripe grain
behind the blinds and teardrops of the sun
bales of hay
bursting corn
footpaths in the noonday heat
beneath the eaves of an autumnal summer

i saw you in the shimmer of leaves clouds and parched tongues
in solemn divestitures after performances
in fragments across centuries of bitter rain
in crucifixions with no resurrections

i saw you in the faces beneath the leaves the thorn the mud
the bracken hope and hunger in our scrambling
the traps and fires of our wanting
and our needing

for you this
for me this
is this all there is

for us under the flowers the altars the ravages of wind

the schools and temples of confusion
for you whose echo is my singing
mortal
immortal
is this all there is

quivering timbres offer arsenic and brine
honour paid
travesty of eyes managed to perfection
mortal my mortal
my sob
my flesh

entombed survivals

(movement five)

It
plies the broken river
the library the office the classroom the bedroom
the leaky vessel of tomorrow

the graveyard announces Its spired presence
the cities the plains where
It
moves in engines roaring
Hiroshima Nagasaki Vietnam
black holes of America Europe Arabia Africa Asia

water of clay in vessels of hemlock
the-house-in-the-grave-the–spire-the-mound
the roadway ahead and behind the gouged high ground
where i stand looking at me in the pathways of possibility
in the civic gift of barren mountains
mounds and monuments grown in the backyard garden
plateau of eternity in the pulse in the rubble
mortal
immortal
is this the apparition i must cling to
hold forever

the lone labourer of lost hours
gazes into the season which is not the season
bare ground
burnt earth
fences solemnizing life-taking property
bleeding poppies
tulips grown on flesh

the worker gazes in the turbulence of oceans

where i walk the conch shell's call
in the tide's legacy of shore and sky
beyond the dreamed of milk of fresh water
where no one wants to grieve
no one deserves grief

offspring of another parting i am
a blesser of crossroads
the heart the smile the naked touch
this dance which dances me

i renounce the wounds
the scars are healed

the sowers of pretext and pillage
the posturers
the procurers
the protectors of deception and tyranny
have been named

entombed survivals

(movement six)

magnanimous creature
creator of compassion
possess me

presence of our bidding
water of being
do not let me go not knowing why
i who know and know nothing
a stumbler behind within without the word

magnanimous creature
you on the other side of the veil
how far more
how many more torn
how many pierced

how many in the malformation of rituals formed
in the rumours of heaven and hell
tortured
murdered
how many formed malformed

beyond the mourners' punctured voices
gravel
shrouds of sleep
scent of hope in swaddling clothes
holy laces beads chalices crosses daggers
urns bread blood wine

enough of sacrifice
sacred curse
time-eater
fragments of bodies

sand in mouth salt in our eyes

between cup and lip
and moments of clay and water
the desert the rock the sun in our loins
pray with me for rain's first shower

for in the fall and swell of this showering tide
we breathe
day and night and dawn and dusk
you and i immortal

mortal

touch this rock
enter this vein
drink this light
breathe this breath
stand mortal
stand immortal

bruised knees and confessions
mass said at noon (or any other hour of illusion)
the purchased trembling of anonymous candles
the wretched echoes from stragglers who come to feed on you
murdered man torn and nailed
body and blood eaten again and again

the straggler the murderer
the priest the murderer
the hymn the murderer
the prayer the murderer

the candles waver and die

outside beyond the tulips and fences
the uniformed protector waits
the officer waits
the commandant waits

the General waits
It
waits

waits in the mandala of lips mapped in litanies
waits in the bugle and drum of hatreds
waits in the crucible
this circle
waits in this birth my death
waits where i break out and i'm caught
mortal my mortal
the missiles of pomp and inferno

the days have preceded me
proclaiming confusion upon clarity
the wind mourns
the child weeps
but here there is only deafness

offerer of water
rain in drought
afloat in voice i move from word to word
these flown moments of my knowing and unknowing

offerer of water
rain in drought
it is an apple-blossomed morning
the spring dawn of our panoplies and performances
the secret places of our breathing

amidst violins and bombs
this morning of Spring
torn veins of the dead

amidst sleep and dream
this morning of our glimmer
dancer and dance

amidst the stillness of sheets loved and dreamed in
amidst moments lost in roadways and schedules
and doctrines of doctrines
amidst the abyss and the clock
and the sinister gaze of passersby quartered and drawn

amidst this emptying filling
the amnesia of sun and distance
has not dispelled the sadness of things lost

there is a stirring amidst the blossoms and stars
the seasons behind the whip the chain the gas the fire the rubble
there is a stirring amidst the blossoming heart
beyond the occasion of towers and obelisks
and ships and horizons

there is a stirring in the stream that flows
in smiles not yet born
the places of another tremulous becoming

touch the night
the short vernal dream of clouds and words
touch this shore this tree this bud
enter

entombed survivals

(movement seven)

enter the drum and the drumming
where flesh meets flesh
and parts again

enter where smiles erupt
in lines of silence
enter where we have looked and seen blinded
the rising dance that falls in us
that falters
falls
and rises in us
the sleeping waking swoon that breathes and weeps and sighs

enter
        earth
        ocean
        sweat
                body one
                not one
                mortal immortal
        enter
                              heat light darkness
                                  absorption   flocculation
                                              decantation
                                              cosmogonies of us

enter night departures
conjuration of figments   lips   eyes
spontaneous and precarious balances

enter
until the light the secret flutter of this passage goes
until the autumn sun descends

until the word and you are gone
enter

O ever enter
mortal   immortal
one
not one
forlorn of night
exposed in light
nocturnal wanderer
one
not one
mortal   immortal

it is the time
the solstice of prayer and destruction
hope sealed in every dreamed-of sea

time of the centre
the slaughter of innocents in the foliate dust of our ruin
time of the springtime flow of vowels and consonants
revelations in grunts and moans
within the hour where we pass
in columns and columns of event
pilings of festering memory that rise amidst the stricken halls
of sinister intent and ceremonies of rehearsed applause

time of the battered dead
unburied
the Disappeared dumped in fields of trampled mourning

entombed survivals

(movement eight)

like the shudder of god they strike
parched feet and bent back in plots of hunger and toil
the guttering lamp of hope drained of oil

they crawl and hiss and roar
they strike in the desert of lunar dreams
venom of meaning unmaking meaning

they echo in the worn stone of cathedrals temples and mosques
between event and event in glory's triumphant stench

between event and event
the plough breaks in rock   shards   dead bones
between event and event
eyes opened in thorns
tongues constricted in the rage of terrible sleep
again and again

again and yet again the wind laments in the precision dance
of medals flags and uniforms
rigid hairs of well-honed hatreds and hurts

a face
a shape
a body looked at
defiled

entombed survivals

(movement nine)

no one returns
no one returns
no one returns
no one returns
no one
no one
no one returns

no one enters the doorway with smiles and laughter
no one walks in the rustle of Spring
the enchanted paths of blossoming green
no one sighs in the arbours and dells of the evening

the knowing heart of febrile lips
is drawn in wounded silence
bled dry in the glare of empires and greed
convoys and heroes

while the wind whips the rising hour in leaps and roars
and skeletal rocks regain their ancient veins
while the grain surrenders and the fields are bare
while the averted eye endures no more its sentence of sight
i hurry past elusive ports and ruins
places i know and think i know
where searching abates in the sudden clamour
of the evening bell

matin mornings

matin mornings in cowpasture days
confession behind wax-smelling altars
dead man
dead cross

the brethren sing sweet Jesus walking Galilee
they hear the slurp and slap of mud in the footpaths of sleep
their cries legioned in sugarcane fields
calypsoes   rum   Saturday-night brawls

confess, rumbles the pulpited ghost breathing
sin redemption eternal blemish

the brethren of little faith confess sun-cursed sins
in need and hard work and unending need

they know how sweet The Name sounds in believers' ears
they confess   unworthy servants   servants scratching empty
palms   they confess

the morning drinks them up and moves on

gently now gently

among the graves the roses the wild-flowers
laughing   tearful   we met
already you and i already dying in a tremor of madrigals
already in flight
engulfed
in flight
one
not one
laughing   weeping

in flight we touch we hold
one
not one
the womb   the blood   the grave   the dream we do not want

do not
we who know the mud the filth the dust
we who deafen the thunder
we who smile   who hold   who kill

gently now gently   i also dream   gently take me
gently pierce me
you the dream i dream   i suckle   i sleep in

changing return

look into my mirages my songs my screams my prayers my babbles
look into my defences my obsessions
take my blood   search for the ire you think has caused this
distemper   find it   teach me to cope   teach me to give
guidance to my children who weep and are not comforted   tell me
why my mistakes hound me all the time   tell me why the promises
i make unmake me   tell me why i watch me dress   i hear me
leave
i see a stranger return

house

unwilled this door swings
in sleep's invisible shadow
where the unstruck sound of
the unwelcome caller forces awake
my sleeping form

i do not want to answer

i have watched from darkening rooms
his passage over bridges and streams
the midday dust that chokes lung
and prayer and tears

i began somewhere in this vague house
layer by layer
membraned in walls and years

in the veil of my blood
a child with searching eyes
traces the columns of a solitary universe
where one by one every totem of my moment
will be removed

this then is a chapel of forgetting
an altar dressed in the vague cloth
of remembering

and it is i the cortege
who bears impoverished
the memory of this ceremony of going

drought

this is a stagnant eternity
thick with raw fumes

a ceaseless ache beats
in waves of shimmering heat
like broken lightnings
in a dead night

scarred arms of trees probe a barren sky
the odour of burnt earth and dying
are the pattern
the grinding wheel in a crepuscular world

the horse caught in the jaws of fanged mud
the wrinkled breasts of bare earth
a bed of bones and scattered horns

voices bringing no response no twelfth amethyst
sing within the skull

is this the seventh plague
or is it the end

there is no one with the white robe
and no sound of many waters

out of the fields of sugarcane blades and scorpions
i have come to this

i will ponder a while
more voices are born

visit

down this footpath of puddles   marabuntas and tumbled greens
my voice is a breath of smoke
under the blazing sky
i do not remember so fiercely hot

once i roamed the morass that wanders still amidst the dams
deep with the tender breath of fresh-cut grass
and fresh-ploughed earth

that was another world where jamoons and semitoos
were forever ripe
where bunches of red pepper exerted strong lure
not the saddening green that chokingly rises
in the putrid land and encroaching jungle
around blackened faces and drained bodies
i hardly recognize

the sandkoker trees are shedding their leaves now
yellow fallen leaves upon their thorn-strewn ground of
fecund sour grass no grazing cow would eat

in some of the fields the sugarcane has been burnt
blackened in the soot of this labouring mud
these people   my people
are still at work
their cutlasses still flashing in desperate need
in the toiling fields of the merciless sun

so many chasms separate us   i with my dreams on the other side
of the horizon
where the winter is bitter
far from this shore and land of singing water
across the distant sands of my childhood play

in the stream beneath the consolation of blue skies
fish and ducks are swimming   as if nothing has changed
but the houses are in ruins
and the young who i do not know
and the old who remember certain versions of me
each day stare in emptiness at the passage of their years
each day fearing each other's growing treachery
and there is nothing i can say
i who once lived and worked here

i will go to the watch house by the sea and listen to the rising
tide
beyond the rot and ruin
the insidious decay in every footpath and dream here

i cannot bear anymore the stories of rape and murder
the brutal anguish of mutual hatreds turned inwards
people hacked and mangled to death in broad daylight
and the begging
tattered children and adults begging for food
in this fertile land of many waters
this land and earth of my birth

i will go to the watch house behind the wall of the sea and
listen
past the sorrow and the rage and the confusion in me
past the ragblown roadless wheezing in the dying of this day
flesh eating bone in the hollows of each evening

across the buckling bridges
today's women   empire's offal   strike their womb's stirring
cursed in labouring birth and and labour until death

the towns are defaced and barred
decrepit prisons against the enfrenzied horror of the street
caged-in dreams of yesterday and yesterday
and of children and hope gone New York Toronto London way

blow softly on them Atlantic   it is the least you could do

blow softly as they cower from each day's drain and glare
and the ooze that distorts the pulsing eye

prepare them
prepare them
prepare me
in the gathering dusk
of this oceaned nocturne
far away

greeting

i begin with your face
veiled abode of speech
where all beginnings are obliterated

i draw points
maps of texture
of eyes
of nose
of mouth
signs where you may be

to begin with your face
is to begin in the supernal mirror
dawn dreamed iridescent
in the retina of our unlooking

your face dissolves me
in defiance of anthems
hot sands of night
curses
benedictions
alleluias in excelsis deo
mantras for nirvana
incense of sad contours

light anointed
the veiled abyss of your gaze
reveals at the eleventh hour
a turbulence of sandalwood and myrtle
a divination of silence and distance
gales and litanies
stone arches
altars

places of enchantment and denial
desire and the immolation of desire
ensouled in me

body rites

(chant one)

for us glance in glance
in mouth in voice
for us touch in touch
corpus sanctus
mouth in voice
corpus sanctum

for us the spume the brine
this bleeding heave of strangled silence
flesh enwombed and torn and woven
in our tongue

for us the embattled dark that bursts in flame
alone unmet waiting
we who plunge into
thrust
devour
re-create each other
dreading each parting

i anoint you in my gaze
you in whose eye lives the eternal moment
i anoint you
Enchanted Clay
miracle of earth   fire   water   wind
let me gaze upon you
before the distance closes in
and i am lost forever

through the ninefold coils of night
the world's sub\terrain silences
the pulse that beats and beats
in the labourings of fences   gates   bugles   drums

the well of night in whose light you breathe
gaze upon me
make me eternal

body rites

(chant two)

naked i come
child
beast
man
beast
beating my breast woman
in the strands of your embrace
calling
calling in the dark
calling

calling
undone in this festival your body my body
our sacrifice
our joy

i come to you child the man this beast is woman
i come to you in grunts in growls in moans

i come to you
forging speech within without the word
rock
sand
salt
oceaned in our joining

i come beating
beating
in the dawning of each leaf
each dew-wet blossom's foliate silence

beating
forging within

beneath speech where you live

i come to you child the man this beast is woman
the unnoticed shadow noticed
stairwell of day plagued by night
steel doors
bars
locks
bugles   drums
the lies which lie and lie
and insist on lying
as they embrace us

i come
        enter
                probe these octaves
    as they beat
                                       enter
                      bless me
                      absolve me
                      devour me
                      create me
woman this beast this child this man is woman

naked i come
i come
i come

body rites

(chant three)

this rock this you this me i live in
this painful thunder
this sky this earth this you this me
this forbidding water watered of our watering
watered in veins of winded stone
our hands smooth silences
weathered in reaching

                                                                                 open
closed
                    closing in the seaswell fall and flow
of our meeting

the anguished cry
the silent beating distance
and closeness

this you this me
this waking naked transient sated sleep
this wonder
this need
this you this me
this pierc\ed body's billowing roar
this endless night of waiting
this endless day
this limbo of reluctant departures
storms and gales and litanies in our meeting
Sacred Breathing Clay
this you this me
this strangled heave of bleeding silence
this waking naked transient sated sleep

body rites

(chant four)

i offer you my breath at your feet
portions from the burning face
of an ancient sun

i offer you me awash in bitter rain
beyond the plots of yield and hunger
an equatorial need

ginger nutmeg pepper
mango soursop coconut sugarcane   see how
they breathe in my blood
beating in the beating of our touch

breathe in me
your body my body our body my body
breathe in me
breathe me in

body rites

(chant five)

in this festival of darkening light
i have made many fires

they glimmer in distant evenings
in the shadowed warmth and cold
of uncertain insistent unrememberings

old embers
a needy heat

the nights are long and far
and between them you and i
other things have happened   but here we come
to touch and feed and heal
in the root of our gaze

my bones ache
and something drags about the confessionals and lachrimatories
of me bearing no deliverance

once i played in the grass
i ate berries and fruit grown
in the footpaths of my dreaming
i drank in streams the earthen flow of hope

i nestle in you
a stranger you and i
touch me
feed me
heal me
rooted in the root of our gaze
away for a moment from the burning labyrinths
the assassin's articulate and ready wait

the columns of bodies too terrified to feel
authority fattened in hypocrisy

we are a disapproval   you and i
as we touch and feed and heal
even as of each other we approve
in yet another trial by fire

body rites

(chant six)

awake now in this darkening sky
across the cities and borders of our dreaming
i resurrect alien mountains and springs
precarious pathways in the loins
and olives of a Delphic moon

i enter anew the ancient stone
the wind and heat and heave of
the shimmering sea of our living
the cliffs and plains of Olympian fears
the peaks of silence in our meeting

the roads are many in this changing light
which maps our touch
and touches our mapping

they lead through shores and tunnels
obelisks and gilded tombs
the vertiginous ground of our embrace
beyond the royal grandeur of museums
in whose shadow beggars and dogs forage

we are where we have and have never been
here where the brightness hurts our walk
within the ruins of centuries and empires
under the shadow of Minerva's owl

crucifixions in pieties configurated in blood and wine
where the anguished echo of moans
indicts the ecstasy of the humbled and the curious
as the sun gleams on the fading cries
of Colosseum killings
in the labyrinths of pomp

the catacombs of glory

we are where we are and have never been
we who look and are looked
in each fossil and bark
each strand of earth that speaks
and shuts us out
each monument of ordered beauty   tyrannical precision
against which we must not be silenced

body rites

(chant seven)

the sounds of this night
are of another time

they rise and fall within our breathing
beyond the sonatas and tombs
the madrigals in alien voices
across the turbulence of streets
and roadways of our passage

they are already memory
something gained something lost
in the departures of our meeting
as we go from place to place
placing ourselves in our unfolding

body rites

(chant eight)

morning comes
in the silence of our unsleeping
a dislodged night
of open closures

morning
it is the morning of you and me
another morning in the moorings
of burnt-out night
on sleep's other side

morning
morning where we rise
in the sighing of mountains and streams
in this unknowing ground of our going

morning of our morning
away from the sorrowing streets of cemeteries
and ruined fortresses
centuries of absolute stone
the villages of another dream

morning
morning of our morning
in the high ground of our gaze
morning beyond the wall of the sky
the lamentations in jubilations
morning in the silence of our unsleeping

body rites

(chant nine)

they have returned when i had thought them gone forever
they have returned
eyes of poison darkening the corridors of my going
the hackers the tearers
the bearers of doom
i once left far away
or so i dreamed
fanged thorns gnashing at the sun
forked voices assaulting my speech

what can i say to you
in whose touch my living blooms
even in this

what can i say to you
here where fearing my own smiling
i fall awake in this unending night

what can i say to you
in whose breath is my breathing
in whose shadow i now also despair

body rites

(chant ten)

must every smile tremble on lips of pain
in this long season whose morning never comes

winter kills bloom and bud each eternity
even in the warm river of our dreaming
and one by one each forgotten hurt
resurrects in pain-drawn bone
in the shroud and vale of our growing

i want to live
even as life betrays each act of life
here in the foreverness of my doing
i want to live

help me as i help you live

body rites

(chant eleven)

the fragile light of my fading eyes
lives in the green stillness
of this woodsmoke tremulous moment
a distant fire in this body's night
the nether awakening
beneath the eyelids of another dawn

in the reign of this rain
which dreams us in its fall and flow
even in the venom of each tainted drop
weeping from the skies of our undoing
i gather light
i gather light again and again
and again and again it goes unwilled and unknown
beyond the finity of the pulse
which beats and beats in my blood

above fire and wind i gather
i gather in the heave and flow of our touch
my pleasure my pain
i gather light   i gather   i must
despite the spectral tongues' fanged smiles

again and again i gather
even as my own fragile beating fades
even as i breathe in the green stillness
of our tremulous woodsmoke going
i gather even as it leaves me gathering

body rites

(chant twelve)

this bone binds me in the knowing of the darkening
    its pain recedes between your hold
    and the unknowing return and departure
    of unknowing sleep
    the bite of treacherous ground in me always

this bone speaks in me within the darkening
    beyond the mounds of sorrow
    and vales of tears that vanish
    and return in the passing
    of the passing hour

this bone beats in me in the ancient drum and jhall
    in meaning unmaking meaning
    in each trickle of our beating
    in these shores of night and day

this bone   flame of my flesh inflamed
    this bone lives above the ashen reign
    of discourses and ships of terror
    lives in the moment of water
    in the watering of our awakening

this bone rises in the uneasy night of sleep
    beyond the pall of closed and closing eye
    beyond the pall of silenced lips
    beyond the pall of unreturning night
    beyond the pall of the brightening
    darkening sun

it sings and weeps past the foot-worn places of this earth
    past the lamentations of prayer and hope
    past the shrines of triumphant restraint
    past the arbors and backyards of ancient play

it sings and weeps and rises in the unknowing sleep
    which dreams us afresh and older in each return
    the wave and wash of each changing touch
    in our gaze in which we unfold

bone of memory
dreaming of timelessness
bone of the hills the mountains
earth to earth
flesh of earth
earth of flesh
path and ground of timedrawn walks and passages
bone of being   beyond

body rites

(chant thirteen)

being in you being out of you
you being in me in every wave
and roar and breath of need
beneath thought
beyond the ceilings of this time
beneath the faltering warmth of this sun
away from the museums of other days
making museums of ourselves

in you out of you in
this body's ancient need
to touch to taste to smell to dream
in open closures opening in
every wave and roar and breath of need
each changing returning day
each eternity in you out of you in
in me
in me in
today in eternity

ARNOLD H ITWARU was born in Guyana and has lived in Toronto since 1969. He is the author of two other books of poetry, two scholarly books on the subjects of power and mass communication, a work of literary criticism, *The Invention of Canada*, and a novel, *Shanti*.